# CONTENTS

KT-116-223

# INTRODUCTION

## Lots of food

Most people eat about ten times their own body weight in food each year. In a large adult this annual food intake may weigh almost one tonne. Of course, the body does not grow and grow as it gains this huge amount of weight each year. The foods are used in many different ways.

Vast areas of land are used to produce our food, by growing crops and raising livestock. The food business employs millions of people.

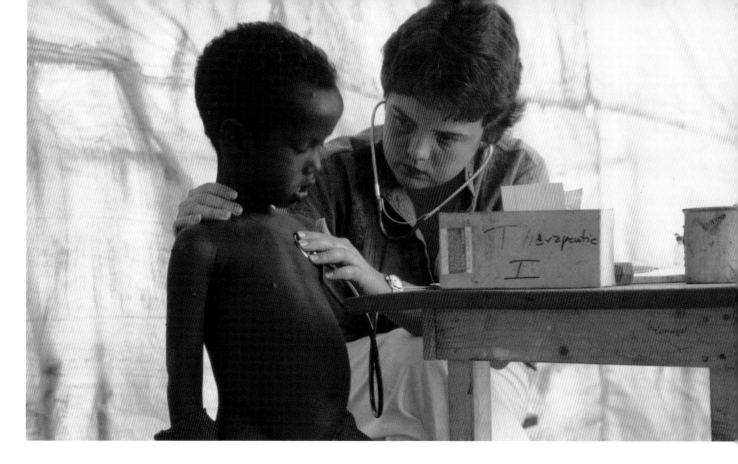

## WHY THE BODY NEEDS FOODS

Some parts of foods are used for energy, so you can move about, talk, walk, run and carry out all other activities. This energy also powers the body's inner processes like breathing and heartbeat, which continue every minute of every day. Some of the substances in foods are used for growth, and others for maintenance and mending. Every day, parts of the body such as the skin wear out or suffer from injuries too small to notice. This is normal, and the parts are replaced and repaired without us realizing. If the body suffers from a bigger injury, the repair process is much more obvious.

Some parts of foods are not used at all. They pass through the body and come out the other end hardly altered.

About one third of people in the world – over 2,000 million – do not have enough food to stay well-nourished. Lack of food brings many kinds of health problems, including an increased risk of infections.

## FOOD AND HEALTH

Foods are more than simply fuel for energy, and nutrients for growth, maintenance and repair. Some substances in food are needed for good health. Without them, the body soon becomes ill. All of the foods that a person eats are called the diet. It's important that the diet has many different kinds of foods, in the right proportions. A diet which provides the body with all its nutrients, and keeps it healthy, is known as a balanced diet. It is one of the most valuable needs in all of life.

# THE PROCESS OF DIGESTION

## Eating and digestion

Digestion is breaking down substances in foods into tiny pieces which are far too small to see, and which can be taken into the body. But this is only part of the whole process of taking in foods. First the foods are eaten by biting, chewing and swallowing them. This is ingestion. The swallowed foods pass into a long passageway through the body, the digestive tract (shown on the following pages). Here the foods are broken apart by physical methods such as squeezing and squashing, and by chemical methods, as powerful juices are added to them to make them dissolve, or turn into a soupy liquid. This physical and chemical attack on foods is called digestion.

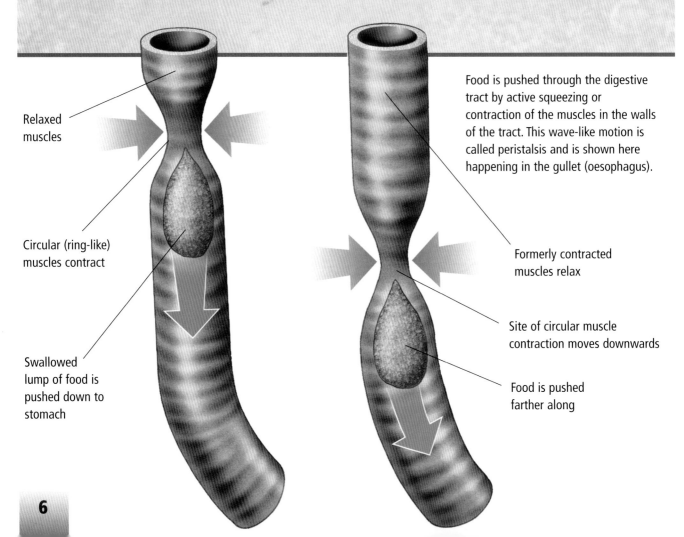

Relaxed muscles

Circular (ring-like) muscles contract

Swallowed lump of food is pushed down to stomach

Food is pushed through the digestive tract by active squeezing or contraction of the muscles in the walls of the tract. This wave-like motion is called peristalsis and is shown here happening in the gullet (oesophagus).

Formerly contracted muscles relax

Site of circular muscle contraction moves downwards

Food is pushed farther along

## TAKEN INTO THE BODY

The next stage is absorption, when digested substances are small enough to pass or seep through the lining of the digestive tract. They enter the blood and are spread around the body. Some parts of foods are left in the tract. Eventually these leftover and undigested remains leave the body at the end of the tract. This is called elimination.

## MUSCLE POWER

When foods are swallowed, they do not 'fall' down through the body. The inside of the body is full of many parts squashed tightly together. This squeezing presses on the digestive tract, like a hose pipe squashed flat. Foods must be pushed along the tract by force. This is done by muscles in the walls of the tract. They squeeze with a wave-like motion that travels along the tract, pushing the foods within. The wave-like motion is known as peristalsis.

## ANIMAL VERSUS HUMAN

In the digestive tract of humans and animals, the squeezing motion of peristalsis is strong enough to push foods and drinks not only downwards, but upwards. When a giraffe stoops to drink, peristalsis pushes the water from its mouth up its neck to its body – a height of almost two metres.

The giraffe swallows water into its gullet, which is angled upwards and raises the water, up along the giraffe's neck, into the stomach in the main part of the body.

## Parts of the digestive tract

About ten body parts work together to take in and digest foods, and absorb the resulting nutrients. These parts are known as the digestive system. Most of them form a passageway through the body, the digestive tract. This begins in the mouth, where teeth bite and chew foods, and the tongue tastes them and moves them around when chewing. Parts called salivary glands around the mouth add a watery liquid, saliva (spit), to make the food soft and squishy. Swallowed food passes through the throat and down a tube, the gullet (oesophagus), into the stomach. This is a stretchy bag that holds a whole meal of foods and drinks, and partly digests it to form a mushy 'soup'.

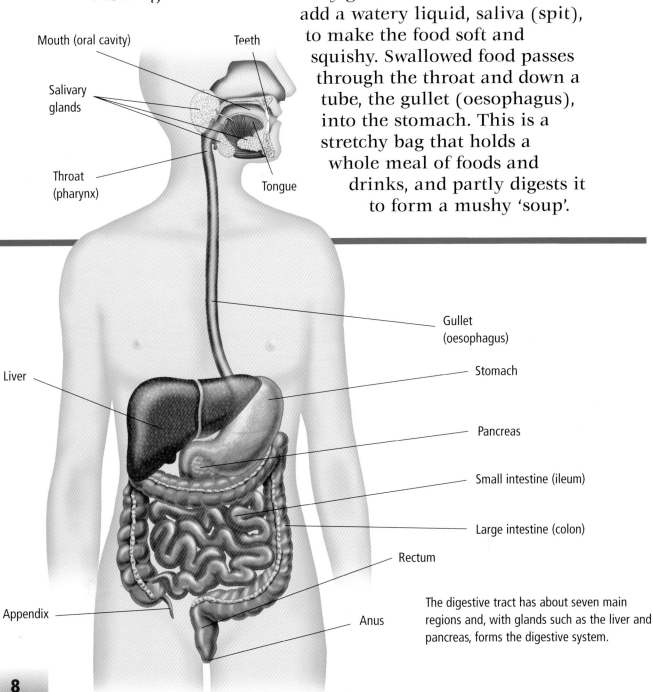

Mouth (oral cavity)

Teeth

Salivary glands

Throat (pharynx)

Tongue

Gullet (oesophagus)

Stomach

Liver

Pancreas

Small intestine (ileum)

Large intestine (colon)

Rectum

Appendix

Anus

The digestive tract has about seven main regions and, with glands such as the liver and pancreas, forms the digestive system.

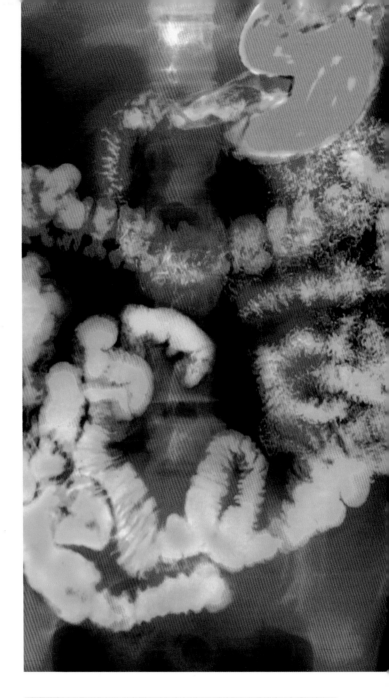

The substance barium shows up as pale areas on an X-ray image. Here it has been swallowed as a 'barium meal' and fills the loops and coils of the small intestine.

## INTESTINES, SMALL AND LARGE

From the stomach, digested foods ooze along a very long tube, the small intestine, folded and coiled within the body. This is where digestion continues and most nutrients are absorbed. The tract's next part is the large intestine, where a few last nutrients are absorbed from the contents, and water too. The leftovers are stored in the next part, the rectum, before they leave from the end of the tract, the anus.

## MORE PARTS OF THE SYSTEM

Two body parts are not in the digestive tract, but they are in the digestive system – the liver and pancreas. The pancreas makes powerful juices which flow along a short tube to digest foods in the small intestine. The liver makes another fluid, bile, which also flows into the small intestine to help digest certain foods. In addition the liver receives the blood which has absorbed the nutrients from the intestines. It stores some nutrients, changes others into different forms, and releases others around the body when they are needed.

### weblinks

To find out more about the digestive system, go to:
www.waylinks.co.uk/series/ourbodies/digestion

## Try this!

The whole digestive tract is more than eight metres long. Use a tape measure to cut a piece of thick string or rope to this length. Can you fold and coil it up so it would fit into your body – without getting tangled?

## Bite and chew

The mouth is the first part of the digestive tract. The front teeth bite pieces off large food items, and the back teeth chew them. (Teeth are shown in more detail on pages 12 and 13.) When chewing, the lips seal together so that bits of food do not fall out, and the cheeks bulge to hold food as it is squished between the back teeth.

## THE TONGUE'S MANY TASKS

The tongue tastes foods so that we know what we are eating. This gives much pleasure as we enjoy a delicious meal. It can also be helpful because bitter or strange tastes may warn that a food is rotten or 'bad' in some way. The tongue's roughened upper surface moves foods about during chewing, so that all the mouthful is crushed and soft. The tongue also helps to shift bits of food stuck among the teeth or lick them off the lips.

All parts of the mouth are involved in eating. The front teeth bite, the lips grip and pull in the bitten-off pieces and then close, as the tongue moves the pieces around for chewing by the rear teeth.

## Top Tips

Make time for mealtimes. Chew each mouthful well and savour the flavour. Eating in a hurry means that food is not chewed properly, so the body cannot digest and use all of its nutrients. Also swallowing part-chewed food can cause pain or even choking (see pages 16 and 17).

## MAKING FOOD MOIST

As foods are chewed, they are mixed with watery saliva or 'spit'. This is made in parts around the mouth called salivary glands. Saliva flows from each gland along a short tube, the salivary duct, into the mouth. The six glands make more than one litre of saliva each day. This is mostly stored until eating begins, when it flows into the mouth. Saliva makes chewed food moist and slippery for easy swallowing. It also contains body chemicals called enzymes which begin to attack certain foods even before they are swallowed (see page 30).

Saliva makes foods moist, soft and easily swallowed. It is made in three pairs of salivary glands. On each side of the face, left and right, there is a parotid salivary gland just below and in front of the ear, a submandibular salivary gland inside the lower jaw, and a sublingual salivary gland under the tongue and floor of the mouth.

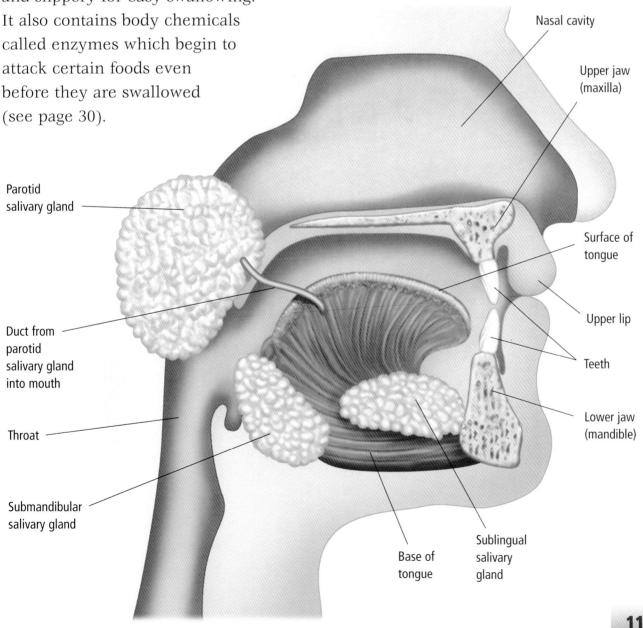

Nasal cavity

Upper jaw (maxilla)

Surface of tongue

Upper lip

Teeth

Lower jaw (mandible)

Parotid salivary gland

Duct from parotid salivary gland into mouth

Throat

Submandibular salivary gland

Base of tongue

Sublingual salivary gland

# THE TEETH

## Two sets of teeth

The human body has two sets of teeth. The first set of 20 teeth grows from about birth to three years of age. They are called baby or milk teeth, or the deciduous dentition. From about six years of age, the first teeth begin to fall out naturally as they are replaced by the second set, called adult teeth or the permanent dentition. They number 32 in most people, although in a few cases, the rearmost or 'wisdom' teeth never grow above the gum.

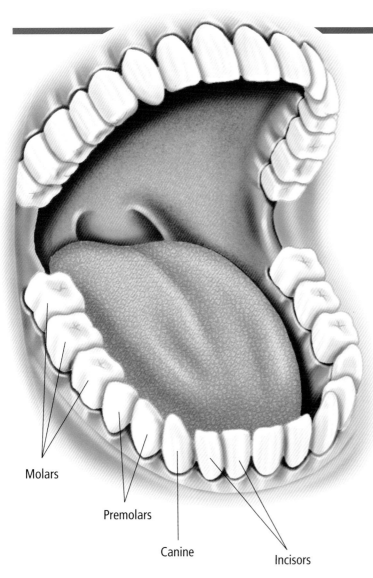

Molars

Premolars

Canine

Incisors

Most adults have 32 teeth. In each half (left and right) of each jaw (upper and lower) there are two incisors, one canine, two premolars and three molars. However in some people, certain teeth never appear or 'erupt'. They stay small and undeveloped, within the jawbone under the gum.

## TYPES OF TEETH

There are four kinds of teeth, in both the first and second sets. At the front of the mouth are incisors, with straight sharp edges, like small spades. These are designed to nibble, bite and slice off chunks of food. Behind them are canines ('eye teeth'), taller and more pointed, for tearing up tough foods. Next are the wider premolars, for squashing and crushing. At the rear of the mouth are the molars or cheek teeth, which are even broader, for the most powerful chewing.

A tooth (this is a molar with two roots) is fixed by glue-like cementum into its socket in the jaw bone.

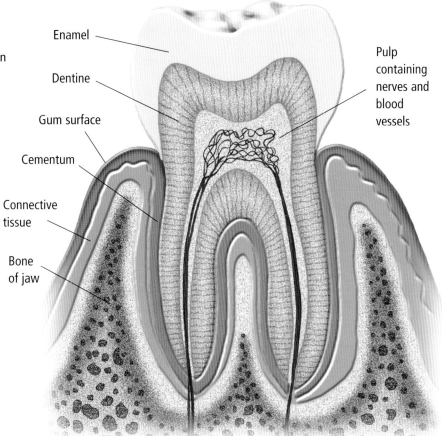

Enamel

Dentine

Gum surface

Cementum

Connective tissue

Bone of jaw

Pulp containing nerves and blood vessels

## INSIDE A TOOTH

A tooth has two main parts – the upper crown which shows above the gum, and the lower root fixed firmly into the jawbone. No substance in the body is harder than enamel, which forms the whitish outer covering of the crown. It must withstand years of rubbing, scraping and wear. Under it is a layer of slightly softer but still very tough dentine. This acts like a cushion to absorb the tremendous forces of crunching into hard foods. In the middle of the tooth is dental pulp. It contains blood vessels which nourish the outer layers, and nerves that feel if the tooth is biting too hard or has other problems.

## ANIMAL VERSUS HUMAN

In some animals, the different types of teeth vary much more in size, compared to humans. In a big cat like a lion or tiger, the canine teeth are very long and sharp, to jab into and tear up the prey.

A yawning lion displays his small incisors (6 in each jaw) for nibbling meat off the bone, and his massive canines (2 per jaw) which stab and grab prey.

13

# DENTAL CARE

## Smile at the dentist

When did you last visit the dentist? Regular dental checks are important for many reasons. The dentist looks around the whole mouth to make sure there are no health problems – not only with the teeth, but with the gums, tongue and other parts. Then each tooth is checked to make sure it is clean and healthy, and growing straight rather than crooked. Some people naturally have stronger, healthier teeth than others – but everyone needs a regular dental check-up.

Various designs of orthodontal appliances help the teeth to grow straight and evenly spaced.

### DENTAL DECAY

The dentist looks for chips or cracks in the teeth, and for patches which might be soft or have holes. This could be a sign of dental decay, also known as caries. It happens when teeth are not cleaned properly or often enough. Old bits of food on and between the teeth go rotten as they are 'eaten' by tiny microbes called bacteria. The bacteria make chemicals, acids, that destroy the tooth's enamel and cause pits and holes known as cavities. The tooth becomes weak, and if the decay reaches

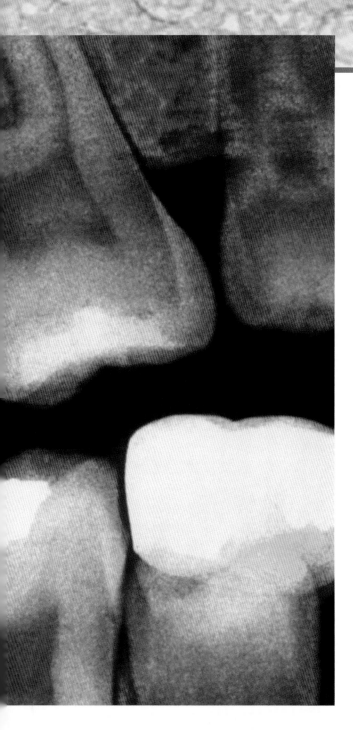

This computer-coloured dental X-ray shows teeth repaired with amalgam filling, which shows up bright white.

the pulp, it affects the nerves and causes toothache. Sometimes the dentist takes an X-ray picture which shows the inside of the tooth. This reveals decay which cannot be seen clearly from the outside.

## KEEPING TEETH CLEAN

To prevent dental decay and toothache, it's important to clean teeth and keep gums healthy, as advised by the dentist or oral hygienist. This is usually done in the morning, after main meals, and always before bed at night. The most important methods are to brush the teeth thoroughly with toothpaste, and to floss – clean the gaps between the teeth with a special thread or tape. The dentist or hygienist will show the best method. A mouthwash may also help, not only for teeth, but also for the gums and the rest of the mouth. As well as cleaning teeth, all of these methods help to get rid of 'bad breath' or halitosis from bits of rotting food.

**weblinks**

To find out more about dental care, go to:
www.waylinks.co.uk/series/ourbodies/digestion

## Try this!

Have you used disclosing tablets or mouthwash? Ask your pharmacist or dentist. Used according to the instructions, they show up or 'disclose' areas which are not clean, in a certain colour. Then you can brush your teeth better!

# EATING A MEAL

## MMMM – SMELLS GOOD!

As you start to eat, your digestive system is busy almost all through your body, preparing for the meal ahead. Even smelling the food, before eating, makes your salivary glands pour their saliva into your mouth, ready to moisten the food when chewing. This is why we say a meal 'smells mouth-watering'.

## CHEW AND SWALLOW

After a mouthful of food is chewed into a soft paste, it can be swallowed safely in small lumps called boluses. We swallow hundreds of times daily, and rarely think about this complex action unless it goes wrong – when we cough and splutter and even choke.

Four stages in swallowing show how muscle activity begins with the tongue and moves down the throat into the upper gullet.

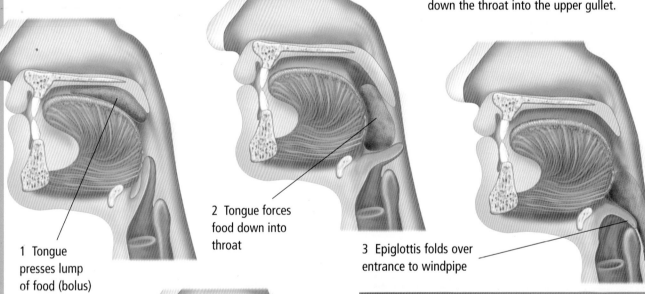

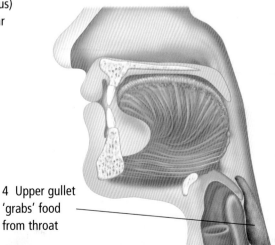

1 Tongue presses lump of food (bolus) to upper rear of mouth

2 Tongue forces food down into throat

3 Epiglottis folds over entrance to windpipe

4 Upper gullet 'grabs' food from throat

## Try this!

Look in a mirror as you swallow. See how muscles move to push food down into the throat and gullet in your neck, by the process of peristalsis.

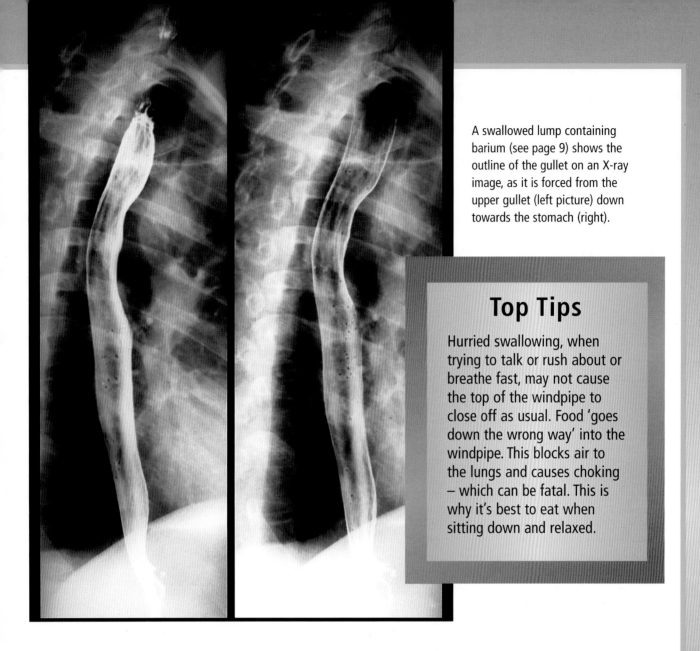

A swallowed lump containing barium (see page 9) shows the outline of the gullet on an X-ray image, as it is forced from the upper gullet (left picture) down towards the stomach (right).

## Top Tips

Hurried swallowing, when trying to talk or rush about or breathe fast, may not cause the top of the windpipe to close off as usual. Food 'goes down the wrong way' into the windpipe. This blocks air to the lungs and causes choking – which can be fatal. This is why it's best to eat when sitting down and relaxed.

Swallowing begins when the tongue pushes a lump of food to the rear of the mouth. As the food touches the rear of the mouth, upper throat and base of the tongue, it begins a reflex or automatic body action. The base of the tongue pushes the lump down into the throat, and into the top of the gullet. Waves of muscle action, peristalsis (see page 7), 'catch' the lump and push it downwards towards the stomach.

## DOWN THE RIGHT WAY

At the bottom of the throat, the opening to the windpipe (trachea), which leads to the lungs, is just in front of the opening to the gullet. When swallowing, muscles in the throat and neck raise the top of the windpipe and lower a flap called the epiglottis just above it, so the two press together. These two actions close the windpipe, which means food has to go down the gullet, rather than sticking in the windpipe.

## 'Down the hatch'

As food disappears from your mouth, it begins a very long journey – about eight metres in distance, and 24 hours in time. Within a few seconds, the mushy, chewed food is pushed down the gullet into the stomach. This is a J-shaped bag behind the lower ribs on the left side. The empty stomach is smaller than a fist, but it can easily stretch in a few minutes to hold more than one and a half litres of food and drink.

## DOUBLE DIGESTION

The stomach continues the physical and chemical breakdown of food which began in the mouth. The stomach wall contains three layers of muscles, and these make it squirm and churn and squeeze the food inside, turning it into a mushy soup called chyme.

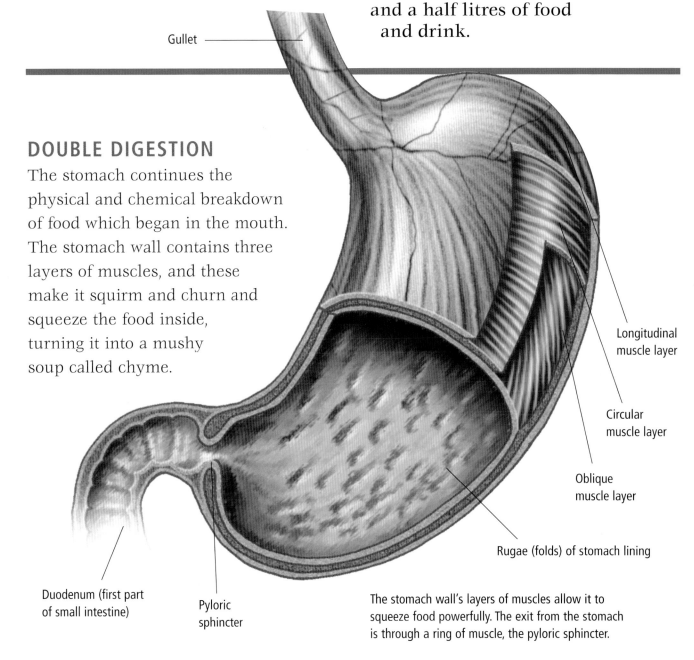

Gullet

Longitudinal muscle layer

Circular muscle layer

Oblique muscle layer

Rugae (folds) of stomach lining

Duodenum (first part of small intestine)

Pyloric sphincter

The stomach wall's layers of muscles allow it to squeeze food powerfully. The exit from the stomach is through a ring of muscle, the pyloric sphincter.

The stomach's inner lining also makes powerful digestive chemicals called gastric juices that dissolve various substances in the food. The juices include a powerful acid, hydrochloric acid, and a variety of enzymes (see page 30). The juices also help to kill any harmful germs that were swallowed with the food. Although the stomach is full of these powerful juices, it does not digest itself from the inside out. It has a thick layer of slime-like mucus which coats and protects its inner lining.

## A LONG STAY

Foods usually stays in the stomach for at least one hour. If the meal contained lots of fatty foods, the stay is usually longer, up to four hours, because fats take longer to break apart.

---

### weblinks

To find out more about the stomach, go to:
www.waylinks.co.uk/series/ourbodies/digestion

---

## ANIMAL VERSUS HUMAN

The human body is designed to eat regularly, two or three times daily. Some animals eat far less often – but have much larger meals. A big snake like a python or boa can swallow a victim as heavy as itself, and then not eat again for six months, as the huge lump of food is slowly digested.

## MICRO-BODY

The inner lining of the stomach, called the gastric epithelium, is dotted with thousands of tiny openings leading into holes called gastric pits. Various cells down the sides of these pits and at their bases make a variety of substances including acid, enzymes, hormones to control digestion, and also thick, sticky mucus to protect the lining from its own digestive products.

This microscopic view of the stomach lining looks straight down into several gastric pits, showing some of the cells lining their walls. In life these would be covered by mucus.

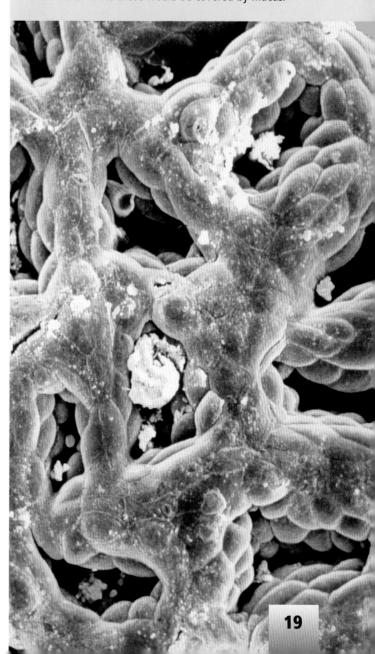

# THE SMALL INTESTINE

## The longest part

The small intestine is by far the longest part of the digestive tract, at about six metres, but also the narrowest, at only four centimetres wide. It is looped, folded and coiled into the lower part of the main body, the abdomen, and consists of three sections. First is the duodenum, about 25 centimetres long, which joins at its upper end to the stomach. It leads to the middle section, the jejunum, 200 centimetres long. Third is the ileum, 350 centimetres in length. The ileum leads into the large intestine, in the lower right of the abdomen.

Liver

Exit from stomach

Stomach

Duodenum

Jejunum

Ileum

Junction with large intestine

The small intestine is 'framed' by the large one. The exact length of each section of the small intestine – duodenum, jejunum and ileum – and the layout of its loops and bends within the centre of the abdomen, vary from person to person.

## A HUGE AREA

Like the stomach lining, the small intestine lining makes powerful enzyme-containing juices to break food into ever-smaller pieces. It also receives digestive juices from the pancreas and liver (see pages 26–29), which also help the breakdown.

## Top Tips

As the body digests a meal, extra amounts of blood flow to the stomach, intestines and other parts. This means less blood is available for other body parts, like muscles. This is why it's wise to avoid too much activity or exercise, like playing sports, straight after a meal.

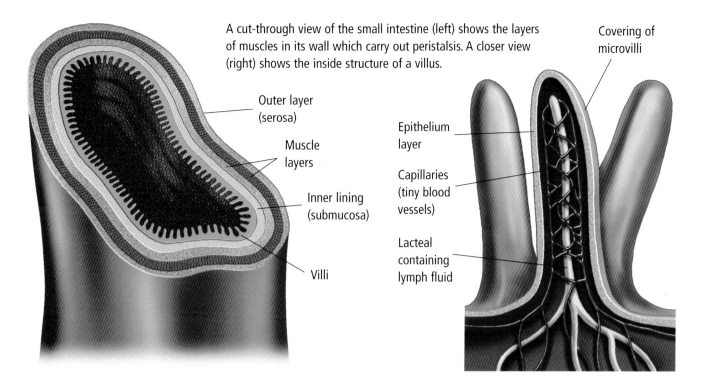

A cut-through view of the small intestine (left) shows the layers of muscles in its wall which carry out peristalsis. A closer view (right) shows the inside structure of a villus.

Outer layer (serosa)

Muscle layers

Inner lining (submucosa)

Villi

Covering of microvilli

Epithelium layer

Capillaries (tiny blood vessels)

Lacteal containing lymph fluid

The small intestine's lining is rippled into folds called plicae. These have thousands of tiny finger-like projections called villi. Each villus is about one millimetre long, and each has thousands of even tinier finger-like microvilli. The plicae, villi and microvilli give the small intestine a huge surface, bigger than the area of five single beds, to take in or absorb the greatest amounts of digested nutrients from food.

## CARRIED AWAY

Nutrients pass from the sloppy liquid inside the small intestine, through the inner lining, into tiny tubes or blood vessels within the intestine wall. The blood carries them away to the liver. Another fluid, lymph, flows slowly through its own tiny vessels in the small intestine wall. It absorbs nutrients too, as shown on page 36.

# MICRO-BODY

Each finger-like villus (shown above) has a covering of many thousands of even tinier microvilli. These are also shaped like fingers but each one is only a few thousandths of one millimetre long. Nutrients pass into the microvilli and seep inwards to the interior of the villus, to the blood and lymph vessels there.

Microvilli (red) cover the surface of a villus (blue area below) and project into the space within the small intestine (yellow).

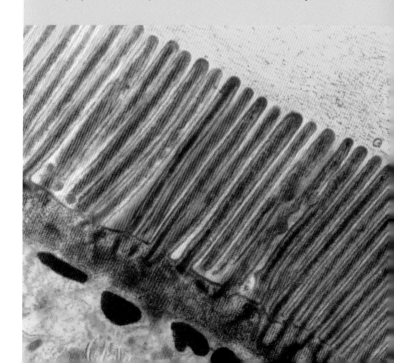

# GETTING RID OF LEFTOVERS

## The large intestine

After the small intestine or small bowel, comes the large intestine or large bowel, also called the colon. It is wide, about six to seven centimetres across, but shorter than the small intestine, at about 150 centimetres. It passes up the right side of the abdomen, across below the liver and stomach, down the left side, and then curves in an S shape to the lower middle of the abdomen.

Flexure (bend)

Transverse portion of colon

The large intestine runs around almost the entire abdominal cavity. Like other parts of the digestive tract, it has layers of muscles in its walls. The longitudinal muscles are in bands called taeniae coli. These contract and pull the whole intestine into a series of bulges, known as haustra.

Descending portion of colon

Taenia coli (band of muscle)

Haustrum (bulge)

Sigmoid (S-shaped) portion of colon

Ascending portion of colon

Caecum at junction with small intestine

Rectum

Appendix

Anus

## INSIDE THE LARGE INTESTINE

The large intestine contains billions of 'friendly' microbes known as gut bacteria. They live here naturally and help to break down certain kinds of

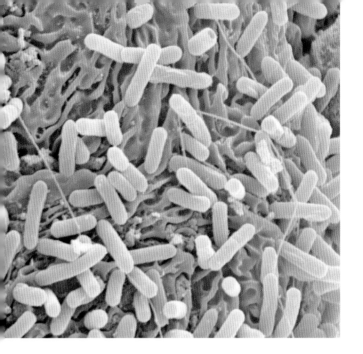

Millions of rod-shaped bacteria, known as *Escherischia coli*, are a normal part of the large intestine's contents.

## THE LAST STOP

At the end of the large intestine, the leftover and undigested contents called faeces pass into the last main part of the tract. This is the rectum, about 15 centimetres long. The faeces stay here until it is convenient to remove them from the body. This is done by squeezing the muscles of the abdomen, to push the faeces through the loosened ring of muscle at the end of the tract, called the anus.

foods, especially plant foods, so the body can absorb the nutrients. The large intestine also absorbs much of the water from the leftover digested food, turning it into squishy brown lumps called faeces or bowel motions.

## THE APPENDIX

The appendix is a small part of the digestive tract, about the size of a little finger. It is at the junction of the small and large intestines, in the lower right of the abdomen. The appendix is hollow inside and links to the main digestive tract, but does not lead anywhere, and does not seem to have an important role. Sometimes lumps of digestive wastes get stuck inside and cause swelling and pain, known as appendicitis. In serious cases of appendicitis the appendix can be removed by an operation.

## ANIMAL VERSUS HUMAN

The human digestive tract may seem quite long, at more than eight metres. But the animal called the manatee, or sea-cow, has a digestive tract more than 30 metres long! This peaceful mammal lives in warm, shallow water near the coast. It feeds on many kinds of water-plants such as sea-grasses, which take a long time to digest.

A manatee can eat more than 120 kilograms of its plant food each day, which is the weight of two adult humans.

# DIGESTIVE PROBLEMS

## Germs and allergies

Tiny, harmful microbes called germs are almost everywhere – even on clean-looking foods. Normally the stomach's powerful acids and juices kill them. Occasionally they cause digestive infection or 'food poisoning'. Also some people are especially sensitive, or allergic, to certain foods, like nuts or shellfish. This can cause problems in the digestive system and elsewhere in the body.

## SWALLOWING IN REVERSE

In some cases the digestive tract gets rid of food by reversing its wave-like muscle movements, peristalsis. The waves start in the stomach and travel up the gullet to eject the food from the mouth, which is called vomiting, being sick or throwing up. Nausea is a feeling that this might happen. Vomiting may happen during an illness, or if the food is bad or rotten or contains harmful substances.

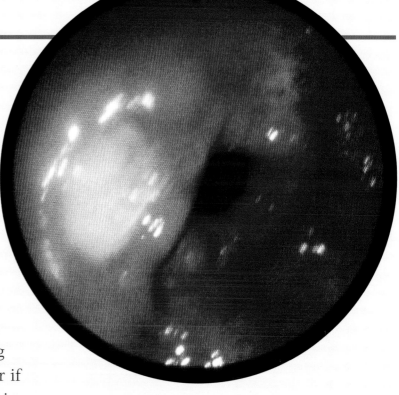

A view through a flexible, telescope-like endoscope inserted down the gullet into the stomach shows an ulcer – the pale oval area. It is like an open sore in the stomach lining.

## GUT ACHES AND PAINS

Pains in the abdomen have many names – belly-ache, gut-ache, tummy-ache and stomach-ache. However the stomach is high in the abdomen, behind the lower left ribs, so pain from lower down is more likely to be intestinal. General swelling, inflammation and pain in the stomach and intestines,

Some fungi, like these fly agaric 'toadstools', have bright colours that warn they are poisonous. But some plain brown or grey fungi can be deadly too.

## Top Tips

It's never worth taking a chance by eating food that could be harmful or even deadly. It's wise to wash dirt and germs off fresh or unwrapped foods, to avoid foods from containers which are dented or cracked, and to check with an expert about picked foods such as berries.

usually caused by germs or toxins (poisonous substances) in foods, is gastro-enteritis. It usually passes as the body defeats the problem, but in certain people, medicinal drugs are needed. An ulcer is a sore or raw area in the lining of the stomach or duodenum (first part of the small intestine) which causes pain and in serious cases may bleed.

Sometimes digested foods pass through the intestines too quickly and emerge 'loose' with lots of fluid, which is diarrhoea. Or the leftovers may become too compacted and hard, and cannot move easily through the last part of the tract, which is constipation.

**weblinks**

To find out more about digestive problems, go to:
www.waylinks.co.uk/series/ourbodies/digestion

# THE LIVER

## Hundreds of tasks

Blood from the intestines, rich in nutrients from digested food, flows to the body's largest inner part, or organ – the liver. It is in the upper right of the abdomen, with most of its bulk behind the lower right ribs. The reddish-brown, smooth-surfaced, wedge-shaped liver has more than two hundred different tasks, mainly to do with metabolism (body chemistry). It breaks down some nutrients, builds up others, stores some until needed, and releases others when their levels in the blood fall too low.

In particular, the liver breaks down harmful substances into harmless ones, which is known as detoxification. An example is the drug alcohol in beers, wines and spirits. The liver detoxifies alcohol so that some of its harmful effects eventually wear off.

However alcohol gradually damages the liver, causing scarring or cirrhosis, so that the liver is no longer able to work properly.

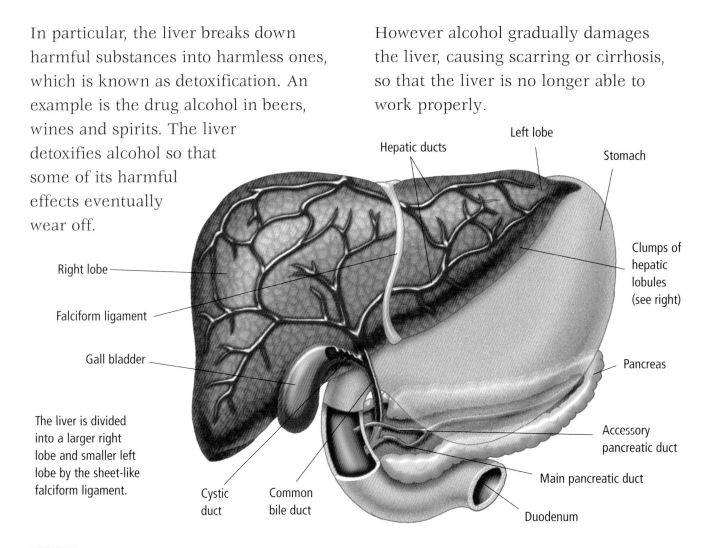

Right lobe

Falciform ligament

Gall bladder

The liver is divided into a larger right lobe and smaller left lobe by the sheet-like falciform ligament.

Cystic duct

Common bile duct

Hepatic ducts

Left lobe

Stomach

Clumps of hepatic lobules (see right)

Pancreas

Accessory pancreatic duct

Main pancreatic duct

Duodenum

## SUGAR AND STARCH

One of the liver's main tasks is to control the level of blood sugar, or glucose. This is the main energy source for all body processes. If a digested meal contains plenty of glucose, the liver converts this into body starch and stores it. As the glucose is used and its blood level falls, the liver changes some body starch into glucose and releases this into the blood. The control is carried out by hormones (see page 28).

The liver contains thousands of six-sided units called hepatic lobules, each about one millimetre across. Inside each lobule are many layers of hepatic cells and branches of tiny vessels.

Small branches of hepatic artery and vein (blood vessels)

Sheets and clumps of hepatocytes (hepatic cells)

Tiny branches of hepatic duct (collecting bile)

## GALL BLADDER AND BILE

One of the liver's products is a yellowish fluid, bile. It contains many unwanted substances, including bilirubin from the breakdown of old, worn-out red blood cells. Bile is stored in a small bag, the gall bladder, tucked under the liver. After eating, it flows along the bile duct into the small intestine. Bile helps the digestion of fatty foods in the intestine.

## ANIMAL VERSUS HUMAN

The human liver weighs about 1.5 kilograms. The world's biggest fish, the whale shark, has a liver that weighs over 1.5 tonnes – it's the size of a small car. The liver is very oil-rich with stored nutrients and helps the shark to float easily.

The liver of a well-fed whale shark may make up about one-fifth of its total body weight.

# THE PANCREAS

## Juices and ducts

The pancreas is a long, pale, slim part in the upper left abdomen, mostly behind the stomach. Like the liver, it is part of the digestive system but not the digestive tract. It makes powerful digestive fluids called pancreatic juices which flow along a tube, the pancreatic duct, into the small intestine. Each day the pancreas makes about one and a half litres of juices. They contain many body chemicals called enzymes, as described later. These attack and break down different food substances in the small intestine.

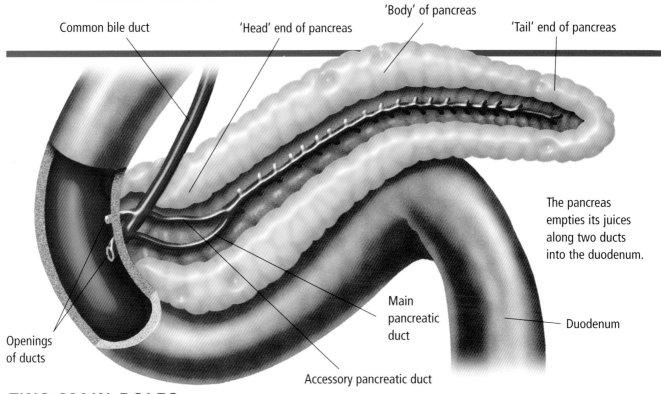

Common bile duct

'Head' end of pancreas

'Body' of pancreas

'Tail' end of pancreas

The pancreas empties its juices along two ducts into the duodenum.

Openings of ducts

Main pancreatic duct

Accessory pancreatic duct

Duodenum

## TWO MAIN ROLES

The pancreas is a dual-purpose body part. In addition to making digestive juices, it also makes hormones. These are chemical substances that travel in the blood and control bodily processes – including digestion itself. In the body's other hormone-making parts, called hormonal or endocrine glands, hormones do not flow along a tube or duct. They pass directly into the blood flowing through the gland. This also happens in the pancreas – only its digestive juices pass along the pancreatic duct.

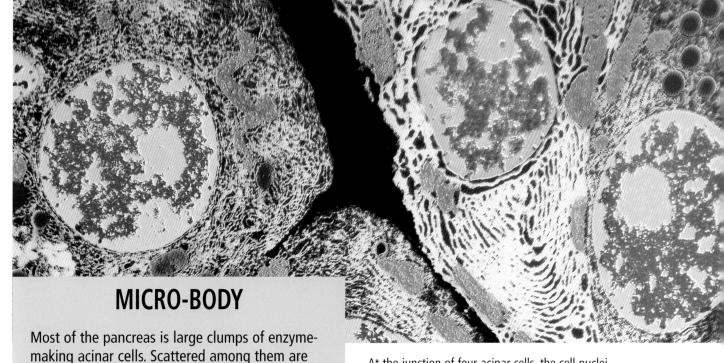

## MICRO-BODY

Most of the pancreas is large clumps of enzyme-making acinar cells. Scattered among them are tiny groups or islets of hormone-making cells.

At the junction of four acinar cells, the cell nuclei (control centres) show up as blue and yellow blobs.

## UPS AND DOWNS

The pancreas makes two hormones, insulin and glucagon. More insulin increases the use of the energy source glucose by microscopic cells all over the body. It also makes the liver convert blood glucose into body starch, which the liver stores. These two processes lower the level of glucose in the blood. Glucagon does the opposite. It tells the liver to change body starch into glucose, and it encourages conversion of various other substances into glucose too, so raising the glucose level in the blood. The two hormones work together to adjust the blood glucose level according to the body's needs.

In diabetes, the pancreas does not produce enough insulin. Some types of diabetes are controlled by eating certain foods at certain times, and perhaps by taking tablets. Other cases require injections of insulin. The condition is monitored by measuring glucose in a drop of blood by a pen-shaped device.

# CHEMICALS OF DIGESTION

## Enzymes

Some of digestion is physical, as the teeth bite and chew food, and the stomach squeezes and churns it into a mush. But much of digestion is chemical. The main chemical substances that the body makes for digestion are called enzymes. They speed the attack on food to break it into smaller and smaller pieces.

Many natural processes involve enzymes. Beer is brewed by tiny microbes, yeast, whose enzymes break down sugar in the liquid, called wort, in the vat.

## MOUTH

Enzymes begin to attack foods even before they are swallowed. Saliva (spit) in the mouth contains a type of enzyme known as amylase. This breaks apart food substances called starches, into much smaller pieces, sugars. This is why, as we chew starchy foods like bread, potatoes, pasta or rice, we can sometimes taste them becoming sweeter.

## STOMACH

The stomach makes two main kinds of enzymes, in addition to its powerful hydrochloric acid. Lipases attack substances called lipids in fatty foods. Pepsins work on protein food substances and split them into smaller parts known as polypeptides and amino acids.

## SMALL INTESTINE

The small intestine receives about 15 kinds of enzymes in the juices from the pancreas. They include more amylases to attack starchy foods, and lipases to digest fatty foods further, into smaller pieces called fatty acids and glycerols. Trypsin continues the breaking apart of protein foods into amino acids. In addition the small intestine's lining makes about 10 further kinds of enzymes to split the part-digested proteins, starches and fats into yet smaller pieces. Finally the breakdown products are small enough to be absorbed through the lining of the intestine, into the blood.

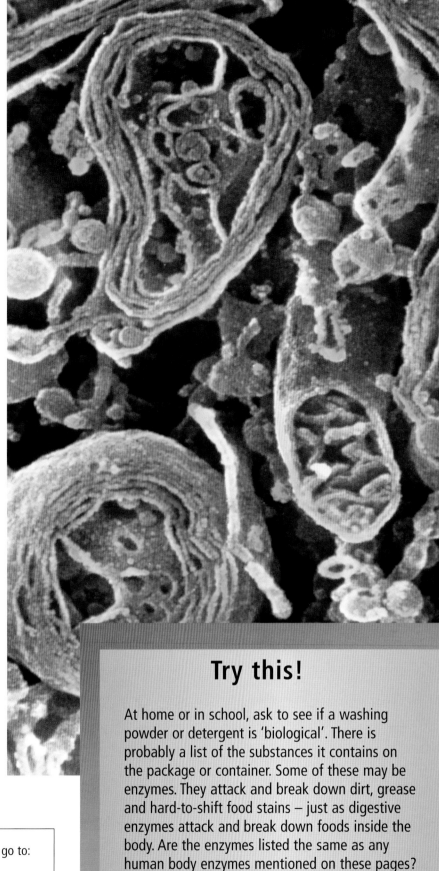

Deep inside a single cell from the lining of the small intestine, are two rounded parts called lysosomes (upper centre and lower left, coloured blue). They make enzymes which break down the nutrients absorbed into the cell, into smaller, simpler substances. (The yellow object at the lower right is a cell part called a mitochondrion, which provides energy.)

**weblinks**

To find out more about the chemicals of digestion go to: www.waylinks.co.uk/series/ourbodies/digestion

## Try this!

At home or in school, ask to see if a washing powder or detergent is 'biological'. There is probably a list of the substances it contains on the package or container. Some of these may be enzymes. They attack and break down dirt, grease and hard-to-shift food stains – just as digestive enzymes attack and break down foods inside the body. Are the enzymes listed the same as any human body enzymes mentioned on these pages?

# CONTROL OF DIGESTION

## Need for coordination

Digestion seems simple. We chew and swallow food – and that's it. But inside the body, the digestive system's many parts must work at the right times, in a coordinated way. Part of this control is carried out by nerve signals from the brain. The signals come from the lower or 'automatic' parts of the brain, so we are not aware of them. They travel mainly along the vagus nerve, which has branches to the stomach, intestines, liver and pancreas.

Pituitary

Thyroid and parathyroids

Thymus (in infancy and childhood)

Adrenals

Pancreas

Ovaries (female)

Testes (male)

Of all the body's hormonal glands, the 'chief' gland, the pituitary, is also one of the smallest.

## HORMONES AND DIGESTION

The body chemicals called hormones (see pages 28–29) also control digestion. Gastrin, from the stomach lining, makes the lining release acids and enzymes, and starts peristalsis in the small intestine. Three other hormones are made by the small intestine lining. Secretin and CCK (cholecystokinin) make the liver and gall bladder empty their digestive juices into the small intestine and tell the stomach to stop releasing acid. GIP (gastric inhibitory peptide) also reduces stomach acid and calms the stomach's churning movements as food leaves it.

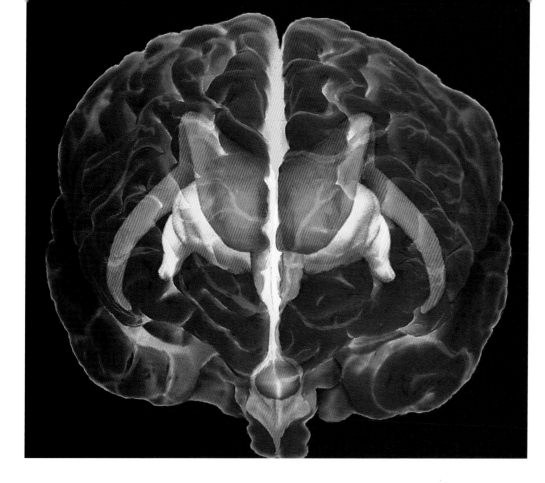

This medical scan of the brain, seen from the front, shows the pituitary as a greenish oval near the bottom of the picture. It is linked by a long stalk to a part of the brain called the hypothalamus, shown in pale green near the centre. The large pink regions are the fluid-filled chambers or ventricles deep inside the brain.

## OTHER HORMONES

Dozens of other hormones control many body processes. The adrenal glands, just above the kidneys, make the hormone adrenaline. It prepares the body for action by increasing heartbeat and breathing rates and blood flow to muscles. The thyroid gland in the neck produces thyroxine, which affects the general rate of metabolism (body chemistry). The tiny pituitary gland, just under the brain, makes about 10 hormones. Several of these control production of other hormones elsewhere, which is why the pituitary is known as the 'chief hormonal gland'. The pituitary also produces growth hormone which affects the body's growth from baby to adult.

## ANIMAL VERSUS HUMAN

The axolotl is a rare kind of salamander from Mexico. Its lake water lacks nutrients needed to make certain hormones, which means the axolotl never 'grows up'. It keeps the frilly gills that other salamanders lose as they become adult.

Axolotls have the body of an adult salamander but the gills of a salamander tadpole, due to the lack of some hormones.

33

# THE THIRSTY BODY

## THE NEED FOR WATER

Imagine it's a hot day, and you're playing sports in the sun. The body will be losing lots of water in sweat, perhaps two litres or more. It's very important to replace this water by taking in plenty of watery drinks. If the level of water in the body falls too low, known as dehydration, then body parts begin to suffer, including the muscles, heart and brain.

## WATER BALANCE

The whole body is almost two-thirds water. Controlling the amounts in different body parts is vital for health, strength and clear thinking. Water moves around and is 'recycled' inside the body in many different ways, so that we do not have to drink huge amounts. For example, each day digestion produces about 10 litres of watery products, like saliva and the juices from the stomach, pancreas and small intestine. But more than nine-tenths of this is taken back into the body, mainly in the large intestine – otherwise we would have to drink huge amounts.

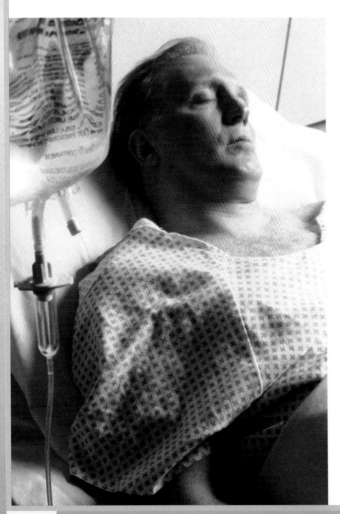

A hospital patient receives vital fluids from a bag, along a tube and through a needle into a vein in the forearm. Lack of fluids for just a few hours can endanger life.

### Top Tips

When the body starts to feel very thirsty, it is already quite short of water. It is wise to avoid the feeling of thirst by taking small drinks regularly. This is better than one huge drink – which can sometimes cause nausea (feeling sick) or even vomiting (being sick).

## HORMONAL CONTROL

The amount of water lost by the body in urine is mainly under control of hormones (see page 28). One of the main hormones is ACTH (adreno-corticotrophic hormone), made in the adrenal glands, one above each kidney. When the body's water level falls, more ACTH is released, and it causes the kidneys to produce urine with the same amount of wastes but less water. This is why, on a hot and sweaty day, the body saves water by producing only small amounts of urine. On a cold day and after plenty of drinks, the amount of urine is much larger. Under average conditions, every day the body loses about 100 millilitres of water in faeces and 1,200–1,500 millilitres in urine.

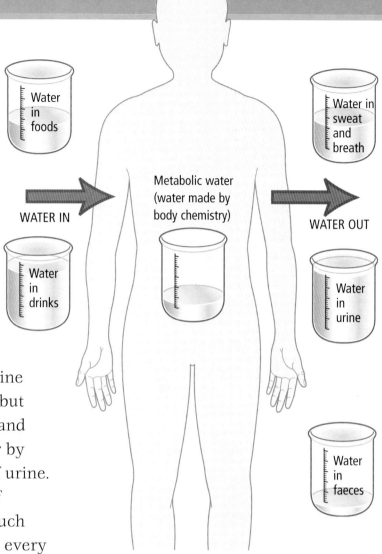

Water in foods

Water in drinks

WATER IN

Metabolic water (water made by body chemistry)

Water in sweat and breath

Water in urine

WATER OUT

Water in faeces

On average, the body loses as much water as it gains each day, mainly by adjusting the amount of water leaving in urine.

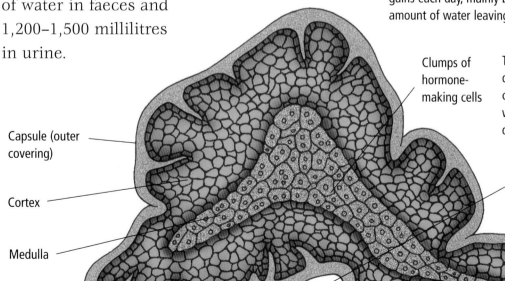

Capsule (outer covering)

Cortex

Medulla

Clumps of hormone-making cells

Base of gland sits on top of kidney

The adrenal gland has two distinct layers, the outer cortex and inner medulla, which produce very different hormones.

# THE LYMPH SYSTEM

## Fluid and tubes

The main place for absorbing digested nutrients is the small intestine. This is covered with tiny 'hairs' called villi, shown earlier (page 21). Nutrients pass into the blood in the microscopic vessels called capillaries, inside each villus. The blood flows to the liver and around the body.

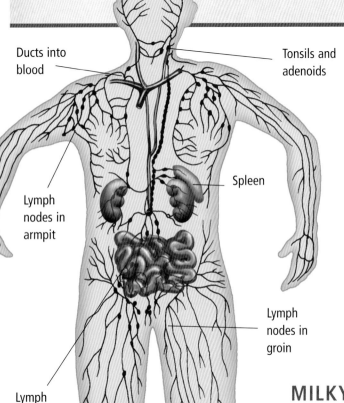

Ducts into blood

Tonsils and adenoids

Spleen

Lymph nodes in armpit

Lymph nodes in groin

Lymph nodes from intestines

The lymph system gathers fluid from the intestines and many other body parts, and adds it into the blood system through the main veins in the chest.

Another specialized liquid inside each villus also takes up digested nutrients, especially fats. It is lymph, and its micro-tube in the villus is known as a lacteal. Lymph from millions of lacteals in the small intestine collects in wider tubes, lymph vessels, which join into the general network of lymph vessels throughout the body.

## MILKY FLUID

The average body contains between one and two litres of lymph fluid. In some ways it is similar to blood – it flows through tubes, carries many important substances around the body, and collects wastes. However lymph is milky-coloured rather than red. Also it is not contained in tubes for all of its journey. It begins as general 'body fluid' around and between the billions of cells in all body parts. This oozes slowly, pushed along by the squeezing action of muscles as the body moves about – lymph does not have its own pump, in the way that the heart pumps blood.

## BACK INTO THE BLOOD

All around the body, lymph fluid gradually makes its way into the open ends of lymph vessels. These join together and become wider, and along with the lymph vessels from the intestines, lead into the upper chest. Here the largest lymph vessels join to main blood vessels just above the heart. In this way the lymph fluid, rich in nutrients from the intestines and also waste substances from all over the body, becomes part of the blood.

## MICRO-BODY

Lymph nodes are packed with many kinds of cells which attack microbes and fight disease.

Cells gathered inside a lymph node include lymphocytes (pink), which are a type of white blood cell, and macrophages (light brown), which surround and engulf germs and other unwanted items.

## LYMPH LUMPS

In some lymph vessels there are small, lumpy enlargements known as lymph nodes. These occur especially in the neck, armpits, lower abdomen and groin area between the legs. The nodes are packed with white blood cells which fight germs, as shown on the next page.

— **weblinks** —
To find out more about the lymph system, go to:
www.waylinks.co.uk/series/ourbodies/digestion

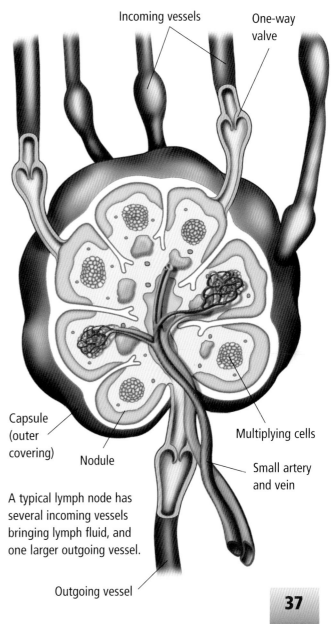

Incoming vessels

One-way valve

Capsule (outer covering)

Nodule

Multiplying cells

Small artery and vein

A typical lymph node has several incoming vessels bringing lymph fluid, and one larger outgoing vessel.

Outgoing vessel

# FIGHTING GERMS

## DEFENDING THE BODY

Cleanliness is very important for a healthy digestive system. Washing hands, using clean plates and cutlery, preparing and cooking food in a hygienic way, and ensuring water is fresh and clean, all reduce the chances that harmful microbes – 'germs' – will get into the body. Microbes taken into the digestive system are usually killed by the powerful hydrochloric acid and enzymes in the stomach and intestines. But sometimes they survive, in which case they are set upon by the body's defence system. Microbes which get in by other routes, such as through a cut in the skin, or in breathed-in air, are also attacked by this body system.

## THE IMMUNE SYSTEM

The body parts that defend against attack by microbes, and against illness and disease in general, are known as the immune system. Its main parts include lymph nodes (see page 37), the tonsils in the back of the throat, and the spleen in the upper left abdomen. They are packed with microscopic white cells, which can change shape and move about to where germs are most numerous. White cells surround and 'eat' germs, or make substances known as antibodies that stick to the germs and kill them.

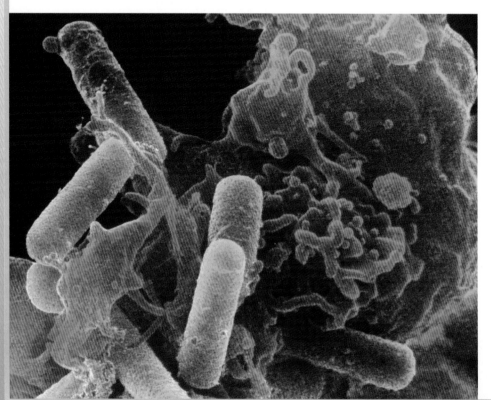

A relatively massive white blood cell called a phagocyte (orange) extends its many complex arm-like 'tentacles' around rod-shaped bacterial germs (blue), ready to engulf them.

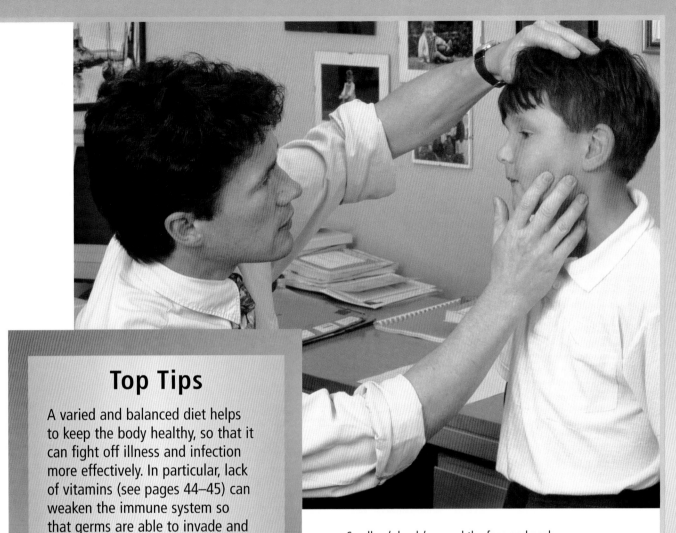

## Top Tips

A varied and balanced diet helps to keep the body healthy, so that it can fight off illness and infection more effectively. In particular, lack of vitamins (see pages 44–45) can weaken the immune system so that germs are able to invade and multiply more easily. This is why eating vitamin-rich foods regularly, especially fresh fruits and vegetables, is so important.

Swollen 'glands' around the face and neck are enlarged lymph nodes and may signify that the body is fighting an infection by germs. The doctor feels for swellings and tender areas during an examination.

As parts of the body suffer from disease, the lymph nodes in those areas become full of white cells, dead germs and lymph fluid. The lymph nodes may swell from a few millimetres across, to 20 millimetres or more, and become painful. They are known as 'swollen glands'.

## IMMUNIZATION

The germs from some diseases can be killed or made inactive, and then put into the body, to make the body fight against them but without suffering the disease. This is called immunization or vaccination. Then, if the real germs try to attack in the future, the body can recognize them and kill them very quickly.

## Solid wastes

The human body produces several kinds of wastes and unwanted substances, and they leave in various ways. One example is carbon dioxide, which is made from the breakdown of glucose for energy, and which is removed in breathed-out air. A more obvious waste is the leftover and undigested foods removed from the end of the digestive tract. They are called (among other names) faeces, bowel motions or solid wastes.

## ANIMAL VERSUS HUMAN

A human body produces 150–200 grams of faeces every day. A hippo produces 100 times more! The hippo eats mainly grasses and leaves, which are difficult to digest. Much of the food passes through the whole system, almost unaffected, and straight out into the hippo's river!

The hippo eats a huge amount of plant food and only digests about one-twentieth of its nourishment. So hippo faeces are very plentiful!

## IMPORTANCE OF FIBRE

On average, 150–200 grams of faeces leave the tract each day. Two-thirds is water. The rest is a mixture of undigested food, bits rubbed off the linings of the digestive tract, and billions

of once-'friendly' but now-dead gut microbes, as mentioned on page 22. If a person eats plenty of the food substance called fibre, the faeces are usually more bulky. This helps the large intestine to work more effectively and the faeces leave the end of the tract more easily, without straining. Fibre is found especially in wholemeal grains like rice and grain products such as bread and pasta.

## LIQUID WASTES

Another obvious body waste is in liquid form. It is called (among other names) urine or 'water'. It comes from a storage bag, the bladder, in the lower abdomen. It leaves the bladder along a tube, the urethra, which carries it to the outside. The action of emptying urine from the bladder is known as urination or 'passing water'. The bladder of an adult person typically holds 300–400 millilitres of urine before its owner feels the urge to empty it. It can hold more, but this causes increasing discomfort, and the feeling to empty the bladder becomes very urgent. The way that urine is produced is shown on the next page.

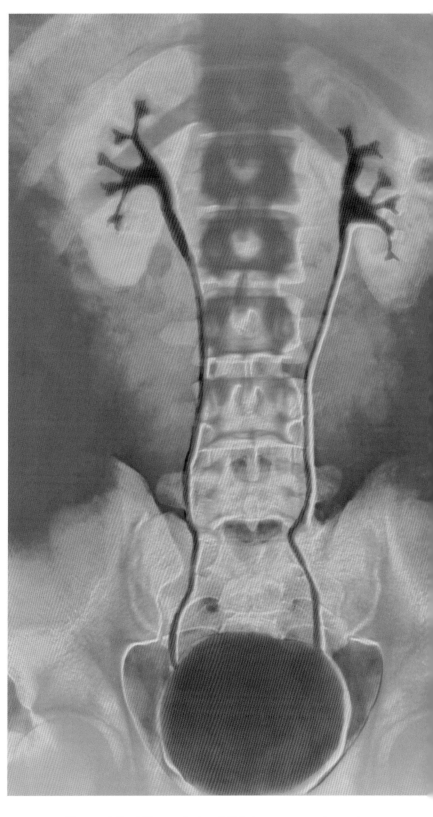

The specialized X-ray called an IVP (intra-venous pyelogram) shows up the urine formed by the two kidneys, and the tubes called ureters leading down to the bladder.

## The kidneys

The body's liquid waste, urine, is produced by the excretory or urinary system – the kidneys, ureters, bladder and urethra. The kidneys are bean-shaped parts, each about eight centimetres long. They are in the upper rear of the abdomen, one on either side. In most people the left kidney, which is behind the stomach, is slightly higher than the right one, behind the liver.

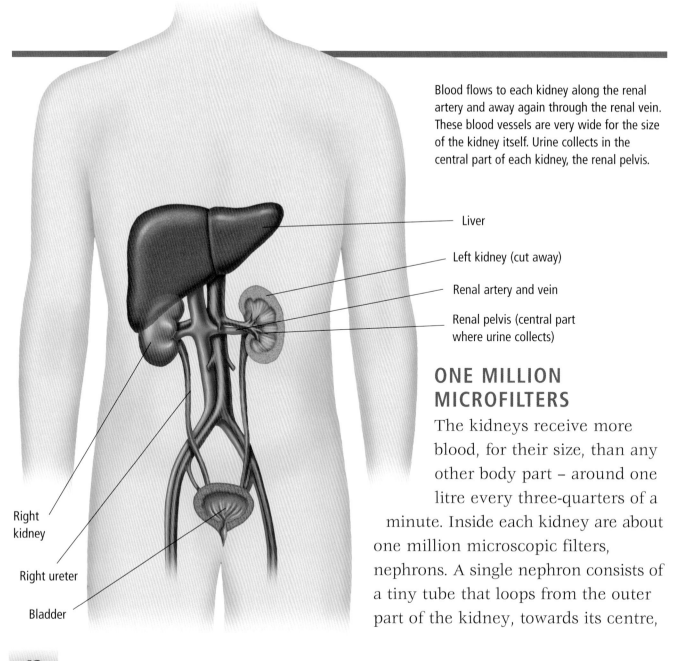

Blood flows to each kidney along the renal artery and away again through the renal vein. These blood vessels are very wide for the size of the kidney itself. Urine collects in the central part of each kidney, the renal pelvis.

Liver

Left kidney (cut away)

Renal artery and vein

Renal pelvis (central part where urine collects)

Right kidney

Right ureter

Bladder

## ONE MILLION MICROFILTERS

The kidneys receive more blood, for their size, than any other body part – around one litre every three-quarters of a minute. Inside each kidney are about one million microscopic filters, nephrons. A single nephron consists of a tiny tube that loops from the outer part of the kidney, towards its centre, and then back again. The start of the tube is shaped like a cup, called the glomerular capsule. It receives water containing both wastes and useful substances from the glomerulus – a tiny knot of capillary blood vessels inside the cup.

This liquid flows along the looped tube, where useful substances plus enough water for the body's needs are taken back into the blood. At the lower end of the tube the liquid, now called urine, flows into the space in the middle of the kidney – along with urine from the other million nephrons. If all the nephron tubes in one kidney were straightened and joined together, they would stretch 50 kilometres.

## DOWN TO THE BLADDER

Urine contains urea, certain minerals and salts, and water which the body does not need. It passes from each kidney along a tube, the ureter, down into the bladder. The ureters, like the digestive tract, are squashed flat by pressure inside the body. But they also have muscles in their walls to make the wave-like movements of peristalsis. These movements squeeze the urine down into the bladder.

## MICRO-BODY

Each micro-filter in the kidney has a bunch-like knot of tiny blood vessels, glomerulus, from which wastes and excess water are removed and then processed to form urine.

The glomeruli in this micro-photograph are coloured blue by computer. The linking blood vessels are orange.

### weblinks⬏

To find out more about cleansing the blood, go to:
www.waylinks.co.uk/series/ourbodies/digestion

# HEALTHY EATING

## A balanced diet

The body needs many different kinds of foods, to stay healthy. There are several main kinds of food groups or substances, and each is important for the body's needs – but so is the balance between them. A healthy diet includes at least five portions of fresh fruit and vegetables each day, such as an apple or banana as a snack, and peas, tomatoes or beans with a main meal, instead of chipped potatoes or 'fries' with everything!

## FOOD AND ILLNESS

Eating in an unhealthy way does not just affect the digestive system, it can cause problems in many other parts of the body. For example, too many foods which are rich in animal fats can cause diseases of the heart and blood vessels. One of the most serious health problems in developed countries is obesity – being overweight, due to eating too much. Obesity increases the risks of dozens of health problems, from heart disease to painful joints. The remedy is simple: eat less and take plenty of suitable exercise.

### CARBOHYDRATES

Also known as starches and sugars. Main use is for energy. Found in bread, potatoes, pasta, rice, and various fruits and vegetables.

### PROTEINS

Important for body structure, to build and repair its parts. Needed especially for growth, and for strong bones and muscles. Found in all kinds of meat, fish, milk, eggs, cheese, and in some vegetables.

Playing sports on an empty stomach, or just after a large meal, can lead to dizziness, abdominal pain, nausea and cramps. The body needs enough food to supply energy for activity – but not too much.

## Top Tips

Many people have a rushed and hurried lifestyle. When time is short, one of the meals they are most likely to miss is the first of the day – breakfast. Yet this is also one of the most important meals. It provides a boost of energy through the morning and keeps the digestive system working in a regular way.

### VITAMINS AND MINERALS
Used in many different ways inside the body, such as keeping the skin and nerves healthy, allowing the production of new microscopic cells for the blood, and helping the body to fight disease. Found especially in fresh fruits and vegetables.

### OILS AND FATS (LIPIDS)
Needed for several reasons, such as to provide some energy, and to build certain body parts like nerves. Healthiest kinds are oils from plant products, like vegetable oils. Eating too many fats from animal sources, such as fatty meats, is not healthy.

### FIBRE
This substance is not digested and absorbed by the body, but it helps the digestive system work well and reduces the risk of disorders of the digestive tract such as colonic cancer. Found in wholemeal bread, pasta and rice, fresh fruits and vegetables.

# GLOSSARY

**abdomen** The lower part of the main body or torso, below the chest, which contains mainly the parts for digestion, excretion and reproduction.

**brain** An incredibly complex part of the body, in the upper part of the head, made of billions of nerve cells and nerve fibres. The brain receives information from the senses, controls the body's movements, and is the site of thoughts, memories, conscious awareness and the mind.

**capillary** The smallest type of blood vessel, much thinner than a human hair, with walls only one cell thick.

**carbon dioxide** A substance formed from the breakdown of nutrients inside the body to obtain energy for life processes, and which is poisonous if allowed to accumulate in the body.

**cell** A single unit or 'building block' of life – the human body is made of billions of cells of many different kinds.

**chyme** The soupy liquid formed in the stomach of digesting foods, which then oozes into the small intestine.

**colon** The large intestine.

**diet** All of the foods and drinks that a person consumes. (This word has other meanings, when eating less food such as a weight-loss diet, or when eating foods of a particular kind, such as a vegetarian or vegan diet.)

**digestion** Breaking down food substances into smaller, simpler parts which can be taken into the body.

**digestive system** The parts of the body involved in taking in, breaking down, absorbing and processing foods and the nutrients they contain.

**digestive tract** The long passageway through the body, from mouth to anus.

**duodenum** The first part of the small intestine, after the stomach.

**enamel** The white or whitish-yellow substance forming the very hard outer layer of a tooth.

**enzyme** A substance that breaks apart or changes another substance into different forms. There are many enzymes in the digestive process and enzymes in other body parts too.

**faeces** Leftovers of the digestive process, which leave the digestive tract through the anus.

**glucose** A sugary substance, often called 'blood sugar', which is found in the blood and many body parts, and is broken apart to give the body its main source of energy.

**hormones** Natural body chemicals made by parts called endocrine glands, that circulate in blood and control many processes such as growth, the use of energy, water balance and the formation of urine.

**ileum** The third and last part of the small intestine, after the jejunum and before the large intestine.

**immune system** Parts that defend the body against attack by microbes, and against illness and disease in general.

**immunity** The ability of the body to recognize germs (harmful microbes) and destroy them before they can multiply and cause disease.

**jejunum** The second part of the small intestine, after the duodenum and before the ileum.

**lymph** Milky-looking fluid from around and between cells and tissues, which flows into tubes called lymph vessels and eventually into the blood system.

**lymph node** Enlarged, lump-like part of a lymph vessel or tube, containing millions of cells which kill germs. Lymph nodes usually swell during illness and are known as 'swollen glands'.

**mucus** General name for various thick, slimy, gooey fluids made by the body, especially to coat and protect the surfaces of its inner parts.

**nerves** Long, thin, string-like parts inside the body, which carry information in the form of nerve impulses or signals.

**nutrients** Substances which the body uses in various different ways, such as for growth, to build new parts and tissues, and to break apart for energy.

**oxygen** A gas making up one-fifth of air, which has no colour, taste or smell, but which is vital for breaking down nutrients inside the body to obtain energy for life processes.

**peristalsis** Wave-like, squeezing motion of muscles, especially where they form a tube or bag and squeeze to move along the contents.

**pituitary gland** A tiny part under the front of the brain inside the head, which makes many different hormones and controls a variety of bodily processes such as growth and development.

**reflex** A quick automatic reaction by the body, to a sudden change or situation which could be harmful, such as blinking the eyes if something comes near them.

**saliva** The watery liquid made by six salivary glands inside the face, which moistens the mouth and pours onto food to help chewing and swallowing.

**urethra** A tube leading from the urinary bladder to the outside, along which the waste liquid urine passes during urination.

**urine** A waste liquid made in the kidneys by filtering unwanted substances and water from the blood.

**vein** A blood vessel with thin walls that carries blood under low pressure back to the heart.

**villi** Tiny hair- or finger-like projections, especially those lining the small intestine.

**vitamins** Naturally occurring substances either made by the body or taken up in food, which are needed to keep the body healthy and avoid illness.

# FURTHER INFORMATION

## BOOKS

Body Focus: The Digestive System, Carol Ballard (Heinemann, 2003)

Digestion and Reproduction, Steve Parker, Kristina Routh (Gareth Stevens Publishing, 2004)

The Digestive and Excretory Systems, Susan Dudley Gold (Enslow Publishers, 2004)

The Digestive System, Rebecca Johnson (Lerner Publications, 2005)

Fueling the Teen Machine, Ellen Shanley, Colleen Thompson (Bull Publishing, 2001)

Staying Healthy: Eating Right, Alice B. McGinty (Franklin Watts/Orchard Books, 1999)

## ORGANIZATIONS

**British Dental Health Foundation**
The leading UK-based independent oral health charity, aiming to help people improve their oral health.
Smile House, 2 East Union Street, Rugby, Warwickshire CV22 6AJ  Tel: 0870 770 4000
Dental Helpline: 0845 063 1188 (local rate)

**Allergy UK**
The national medical charity established to increase understanding and awareness of allergy, including food allergy, also to help people manage their allergies, to raise funds for allergy research and to provide training in allergy for health care professionals.
Deepdene House, 30 Bellegrove Road, Welling, Kent DA16 3PY  Tel: 020 8303 8525
Allergy Helpline: 020 8303 8583

**National Kidney Federation**
The only UK charity run by kidney patients for kidney patients, aiming to promote the welfare of persons suffering from kidney disease or renal failure and those relatives and friends who care for them.
6 Stanley Street, Worksop S81 7HX
Tel: 01909 487795
Helpline: 0845 601 02 09

# INDEX